בס"ד

This book belongs to:

לה׳ הארץ ומלואה

Please read it to me!

Hachai

My Jewish ABC's

By

DRAIZY ZELCER

Illustrated by

PATTI NEMEROFF

Hachai

PUBLISHING

Dedicated to
Sarah and Yitzchak Sheinkopf
May your lives always be filled with Torah
and with love for every Jew.

Debra and Henry Sheinkopf

✳ ✳ ✳

My Jewish ABC's

Dedicated to Suri Holtz (Apfelbaum) A"H who taught me
so much in her short lifetime. Love, Draizy

Dedicated with joy to the marriage of Jocelyn and Robert. P.N.

First Edition - August 1994 - Elul 5754
Second Impression - November 1996 - Kislev 5757
Third Impression - January 2001 - Tevet 5761
Fourth Impression - July 2003 - Tammuz 5763

Copyright © 1994 by HACHAI PUBLISHING
ALL RIGHTS RESERVED

Editor: D. Rosenfeld

ISBN: 0-922613-62-1
LCCN: 93-81028

HACHAI PUBLISHING
Brooklyn, N.Y. 11218
Tel: 718-633-0100 Fax: 718-633-0103
info@hachai.com - www.hachai.com
Printed in China

Aa

A is for AFIKOMEN
That Ari can hide.
This Pesach he'll ask
For an airplane to ride.

Bb

B is for BUBBY
Who mixes and bakes,
Blueberry buns
And beautiful cakes.

Cc

C is for CANDLES
Which Mommy will light,
As she covers her eyes
Each Friday night.

Dd

D is for DREIDEL
Which Dina did spin.
Poor little darling -
It dropped on a shin.

Ee

E is for ESROG
Which grows on a tree.
It's bumpy and yellow -
Can everyone see?

Ff

F is for FRIDAY
When four friendly fish,
Are frying to be
A fine Shabbos dish.

Gg

G is for GRAGGER -
The greatest of toys.
Goldie's got a green one
That makes a lot of noise.

Hh
H is for HAVDALLAH candle -
Hindy holds it high.
When Shabbos is over,
It's hard to say good-bye.

Ii I is for INK
In which the Sofer dips his quill,
And writes a Torah scroll
With care and with skill.

Jj

J is for JEWS
Jumping for joy.

Simchas Torah's fun
For a Jewish girl and boy.

Kk

K is for KIDDUSH -
Kalmen sings it line by line.
Then he makes a brochah
On a cup of kosher wine.

Ll

L is for LULAV
Which Leah lifts with pride.
She loves to shake it
                    up and down
And then from side to side.

Mm

M is for MEZZUZAH
Mounted on the door,

Of Malky's house, and Motty's school,
And Uncle Moishy's store.

Nn

N is for NAPKIN
Which Nosson so neat,
Tucks near his neck
Before he will eat.

O is for OLIVES
Which grow on olive trees.
We make olive oil for Chanukah
By giving them a squeeze.

Pp

P is for PENNY
That Penina puts away,
To place inside her pushkah
Every single day.

Qq

Q is for QUIET -
We quickly do our best,
To quit making noise
When our parents want to rest.

Rr R is for ROOSTER
Who crows so loud to say:
Jump out of bed and thank
Hashem
For this brand new day.

Ss S is for SIDDUR
With which we start each day.
First we say our prayers,
And then we run to play.

Tt T is for TORAH -
On tiptoes Tuly stands,
To touch and kiss it gently
With his tiny little hands.

Uu

U is for UMBRELLA
Which Uri holds up high,
To share with Uncle Uzi
Until the rain goes by.

Vv

V is for VEGETABLES
We eat on Pesach night.
Morror's very bitter
So we take a tiny bite.

Ww

W is for WATER
With which we wash our hands,
When we wake up
every morning
As the Torah way commands.

Xx

X is EXTRA special -
Like the tzedakah father gives.
He's an eXcellent eXample
Of the way a good Jew lives.

Yy

Y is for YARMULKA-
Like the one on Yossi's head.
Yehuda has a yellow one,
And Yonasan's is red.

Zz Z is for ZEMIROS -
When Zaidy sings a song,
Zevi and Zahava
And Zalmy sing along.